Foray

Border Reiver Women

Pippa Little

Biscuit Publishing

Published 2009 © in Great Britain

Biscuit Publishing Ltd
PO Box 123, Washington
Newcastle upon Tyne
NE37 2YW

www.biscuitpublishing.com

Copyright © Pippa Little 2009
All rights reserved

ISBN 978 1 903914 35 9

Front cover artwork: *Wall Near Housesteads*
©2009 Christina Mingard www.hawthorncottageindustry.co.uk
Cover Design and Typesetting by Colin Mulhern

Pippa Little was born in Tanzania, brought up in Scotland and has settled in Northumberland with her family. She has won an Eric Gregory Award, a Royal Literary Fund menteeship (2006), the Biscuit International Poetry Prize (2008) and the Andrew Waterhouse Award (2009). She was a poetry editor of *Writing Women* and two Virago anthologies. Her poems have been widely published in magazines and anthologies. *The Spar Box* (Vane Women) was a PBS Pamphlet Choice (2006).

Foray
Border Reiver Women 1500~1600

In the sixteenth century the lands surrounding the Scots/English border resembled a war zone. Though Borderers were descended from the same stock, spoke much the same language and had more in common with each other than with those living in London or Edinburgh, political interests instigated wars of aggression which kept them at each others' throats.

Violence created poverty and raiding became a means of survival. The words 'bereave' and 'blackmail' came into our language through the actions of the Elliotts, Armstrongs, Charltons, Kerrs, Scotts and many other riding names, including the Littles. Though Wardens were appointed to dispense the law across the Western, Eastern and Middle Marches, these men were often corrupt and justice was more likely to be found by the reivers taking matters into their own hands.

For women on either side of the Border life was extremely hard. Farms and smallholdings could not sustain families, but it fell to women to raise children, grow crops and keep animals. There would be continual raids or forays when their sheep or cattle would be stolen along with anything of value, even pots, pans and coats. Their own men folk would often be gone on raiding expeditions and either returning wounded or not returning at all. Rape, though seldom mentioned in contemporary accounts or subsequent studies, would have been a common reality. Feuding between families was also widespread, with bloody reprisals and counter-reprisals.

Alastair Moffat comments on a duality of opposites running through the long story of the Borders: that its extremes of landscape, from bleak, windswept hill country to douce green fields and 'knowes', echo the dour and taciturn, almost silenced, will to endure that co-exists with a love of words, a love of singing, of the voluble and imaginative, which came to a flowering in the Border Ballads.

Not much has been written about the women of the reiving communities in comparison with their men. Yet it's widely accepted that women were keepers of the Ballads, that through the very worst of times they kept them alive. These poems add their singing to that chorus.

In Memory

of Meg Laidlaw, the mother of James Hogg, Janet Scott of Sandyknowe Farm, Nancy Brockie of Bemersyde and all the women who were the major sources of the Border Ballads, tradition-bearers, transmitters of their songs and stories.

Acknowledgements

Other Poetry, Staple, Orbis, Acknowledged Land, The Interpreter's House, Scintilla, Obsessed With Pipework, Magma.

The author would like to acknowledge the financial support of a New Writing North 'Northern Writers Award' supported by The Leighton Group.

Thanks to

Sean O'Brien, Paul Batchelor, Gillian Allnutt, Bob Little for Everything (including many happy days exploring pele towers, bastles and churchyards!) Brother Harold for his hospitality at Shepherd's Law Hermitage where several of these poems began, Theo Little for ICT help and all the women from Inside Out, Writhen and elsewhere, specially Eliane Mayer, Louise Hislop, Carlotta Johnson and Anna Woodford. Thanks to Jeanne MacDonald for introducing me to Dorothy Dunnett's *The Lymond Chronicles!*

Contents

Who   9
Who
The Cheviots
Alicia Unthank's Ark
Hunterheugh Crags
Coming Back Alive
My Davey
The Robsons Gone
Truce Day

Hush Ye Hush Ye   19
Hush Ye Hush Ye
Northerly
Spinning The Sea
Bonny Man Sandy
Flight
Nine Month Dream

Eyebright   27
Eyebright
Mantling
Wake
Howlet Stone
Old Bewick
Shame Go In Thy Company

Elsdon Churchyard   35
Elsdon Churchyard
On Hopeburn Haugh
Book Of Esther
Swifts
Our Lady Of The Midden
My Minnie

Catcleugh, January   43
Catcleugh, January
The Singer At Low Roses Bower
Left Handed Kerr
Earth To Earth
Foray
First Light
Love, Love Decays The Body

Bird Cherry 51
Bird Cherry
A Death By Drowning
The Ash And The Alder
Kenspeckle
Eggshell
Heron
Spur
Evestones

Wild, Perpetual Voice 61
Wild, Perpetual Voice

Notes 66

Sources 70

Pippa Little

Who

Foray

Who

Who by Hollows Tower
Who by treachery
Who by Angerton
Who by butchery

Who by circumstance
Who by power
Who by hunger
Who by feud and spur

Who by Spadeadam Waste
Who by thievery
Who by Tushielaw
Who by bravery

Who by splent and sword
Who by leather jack
Who by the Bold Buccleuch
Who by the Galloway's back

Who by ride and reive
Who by Hesleyside
Who by Redeswire
Who by blade abide.

The Cheviots

are a long, darkening room, unswept

as if men who came hungry
cleaved its hearthstone with their axes,
tore cloth from skin, skin from bone,
departed bloody-handed

but it was winters and a northern wind
rived down the roof beams, softened and rotted them,
and evening shadows over Alwin water
that kissed the lichens and tussocks
an ashy grey on dead beasts' backs:

home, with stones in it for potatoes, drove roads
a gleam of leavings: carcass bones, the dropped blade
from a hand that will not fist again.

And then in the dim, smudged mark that might be a window yet,
chairs are set so the dead might sit, lit by an ember
whispered into being by a woman's breath.

Alicia Unthank's Ark

They stuffed me in
like an old coat, not folded or bundled
but a bird, trussed,
a raven cut down from the sky,
neck snapped, wings broken back
all snarled and trampled,
made of me grave-goods:

blind and mute but not deaf
to their voices, footsteps
doing their foul work,
upside down I flew
to the well's dark end,
bottom of the world or its beginning:

while our door
cried its broken hinge
in the north wind,
and you came at last to drag me out
wailing the breath of a drowning soul,
a child new-cut from the caul.

Hunterheugh Crags

Rain from the south
we turn our backs on,
feet sore and hands cold,

for the high moor is a running stain of brown in red.
The buzzard looks down and sees us small.
We are rowing our coracle across the open,

for islanded stones worn slant, a landing.
We are rowing towards the human,
the breast we knew once, a cup to call death by.

Coming Back Alive

In deeps of winter, the drift roads disappear
beneath frost-melt, dark's from dawn till dusk,
wind-hunger knotting in the chimney's throat ~

nothing else
but to sing and to spin,
feed the hearth its peat,

offer thin broth and pity the beasts
flank-deep in snow,
unchanging as stars.

Each winter longer than the last, frail bridge
between our horsemen fallen silent,
the blue coughing of our children and the far

hoof beats from another time,
not yet, but travelling towards us.

My Davey

The book o' bosom priests, what do they remember~
tramping mud roads, a bite and a bed, some lass's face
or two knuckles on his Bible, a bauble instead of a ring?

I have smell of the woods, skin-scents of bog myrtle,
betony, of sunlight flooding the cold hills with sloe wine
and wild honey, your hands hard-grooved and smooth
as leather to my flesh, whoosh of the words from your mouth
lifting and swaying the hairs on my neck like wheat;
hot thump of my heart;

I have the stumble of the Linhope Spout, its flash of cold grace
that day we stood breathless and naked in it: I have,
through the wind and the rain and the low fog,
my own rough shelter of the cattle's necks,
warmth of their breath sweet as yours,
when I come in.

The Robsons Gone

They went to keep the tryst
seven nights since and are not returned.

I watch the hills until my eyes itch shadows
that will not turn into human shapes.

Such quiet around us now they are gone,
and hunger stalking our skirts.

They were bound for the border
mustering Milburns on their journey

now their hoof beats' echo
is an ash beaten by the wind, or only

thudding of my heart.
Each day is a stone added to my back

as I sweep and mend and nurse the fire.
Come home, whisper the flames. *Come home*

come home call the birds, from farther
and farther away.

Truce Day

Hard-bitten, aye: by loss
and sorrow, those scavengers.
There's only sleep keeps a truce.
In men's dreams, spilled blood dries,
it's drink that runs over.

And yet~
foot follows foot along the path to where
flags leap, tethered ponies eager for the gallop,
footba' and races run for a silver bell,
kissing and punches and long-lost faces!
Just one day, fat as a trout tossed up from the burn
into our open hands, both buttered and salted,
even the spine-bones sweet.

And yet, and yet,
my mouth's sour
with its tin spoon taste of rain.
Trouble stumps along beside: they say
it's Sandy's Tom to hang,
some laying bets already on his neck.
The old unbridled fear, bitter
to the quick, comes up in me,
but how I love the dancing!

Shadows on the skyline; enemies surround us,
look out from our own eyes.
To babies heavy-headed, dandled on a shoulder,
someone's singing lullabies,
old songs of killing.
How many times
have I seen flesh mend until the scars
seemed trespass on it? *Safe*,
safe, I mutter it under my breath:
yet~ someone is singing.

Foray

Hush Ye Hush Ye

Hush Ye Hush Ye

Hush my hinny, hush my dear
shut your eyes so true and clear
let the wind roar here and by
I'll hold you fast, there's naught to fear

Hush my babe, hush my pet
your father will be coming yet
with meat and gear and warm blue plaid
I hear him riding through the beck

Hush my bonny, hush my lamb
I'll not let live a single man
would skaith you, my beloved one,
while your mother I still am.

Northerly

The north wind crows in the chimney,
stirs the fire's dimming smoulder.

Nobody hears it but me,
the cry of my long life.

They're singing songs,
stirring the rushes as they wheel and dance,

an arm around a waist, a sly kiss
when no-one's looking.

How it was, how it was
my nuzzle, my hinny,

our snatched hours, how quick
I melted, sizzled, butter in the pan

and you, and you, strong over me~
they think they'll never be old,

sat, like me, with the dog's nose in my lap,
that I'm done with love's headlong jig~

the making and the burying of bairns,
all blood bled now,

my body clean as a reed
and hollow for the wind to go through.

Spinning The Sea

She's cleaned the wool
combed it ruly
twirled from the spindle
to a single twisty strand
so many miles of a road to make

round, round, over,
over the moor and over the hills
quick as an adder
lightly-shod as water

no maps nor milestones
only scent of salt
and the blue-green circles spun by swans
drawing her to the edge of the world,

how it runs on farther

Bonny Man Sandy

When you dance you laugh,
your heels crack blue sparks.
My heart's comb overspills with honey,
my own heels start the floor singing, I can't help it.

They say *howay man*, let's see you dancing,
knowing we've got nowhere else
to hold each other so : no place or time.
So we lace our hands and turn

hip against hip then twist,
suddenly your scent's in my hair
as it streaks across your face, my breath
sweet and sweaty at your neck,

so near we are blind to one another
except in touch, a sway of the waist,
my arms around you ~
a *there now, there now*

for after we'll be shifty, shy
and, said or swallowed,
any word will seem too reckless.

Flight

In the dark, alone,
I arched my back against a thorn.
She flew from me like an arrow true,
my little one.

Heartwood is dark, gone,
but sapwood's fair:
my little one was but half a year
and her life was done.

Heartwood is dark within, he said,
sapwood pale as a wild briar rose:
one flies far when the north wind blows,
one buries itself in the secret bed.

Split and stretched, it
does not forget as the body forgets.
Heartwood mourns, he said,
but sapwood sings.

Nine Month Dream

Black winter. The men
underfoot and quarrelling. They'd got
a hind, cut her open. Some thought it ill omen.

I've long been waiting,
turning to iron
a bell tongue-clamped

but last night I lifted up my skirts and ran
strong-legged to the big sky,
ran myself thin all the way to the wood

and this morning wake curled
on its rustling floor, washed in gold
for she's stolen close, light-footed,

cupping my spine with her belly to make
heat that spreads rosy as sunrise. I slow
my breathing to meet her. She smells

of resins, of my mother's hair.
Near to her time she has run
here to lie with me

and we comfort each other
as after rain shoots of grass
do, together.

Foray

Eyebright

Eyebright

Toward evening
rain will come from the west

gathered in a snail-shell's
neat pearl thimble,

resting in cups of eyebright,
settling on button stones and sprung moss;

pleasing rain, with the scent of thunder in it
from the next valley

where a bed sheet lies unfolded on a hedge,
Noah's ship, box-like, above the waters.

Mantling

Kind bird, my John's companion
these fifteen years: a man's head goes grey

but a hawk's red wing-ends stay the same
though both John and she go slower now,

one on the earth, the other in the air.
She brings us snippets for the pot,

good, steady hunter. Company in her way,
the swivel of her eye, the tinkle of her bell:

how she stays close but not too near,
like the dogs, watching over us.

Rewarded with her own share, a chick
or rabbit haunch, she guards it with wings

over her head as she feeds,
'mantling', and it's true

how she makes herself a cloakish waterfall of feathers,
a private redoubt. She does not want or know us there.

I'd trade the flying, all its show,
for that.

Wake

Clay cold the sheet,
stone for a pillow:

who will warm him
in that perishment of snow,

every night and all~
skin for skin! All that a man has

he will give for his life!
What can I give

that he needs
on this journey?

The candle gutters and goes still.
How many miles is it there

and home again?

Howlet Stone

In the gaps, grace.
Godly stump, pellet of newborn's bone.

A soft bell to whisper its dead,
feather by feather.

Who is calling from a long-ago lifetime
for the lamb to come home from the hill,

for something broken to be
mended
or come to rest.

Old Bewick

O earth, cover not my blood,
Let my cry find no resting place
                              (Ecclesiastes)

Stone cross at the road's end
in March rain, cold-hearted~

fell or lain
under daisies' screwed-up faces,
whickens and clarts, hare-
dottle and lichens'
trespass~

his unblinking
turns to slant red hills
running in streams

and lambs supplicant between the knees
of sodden mothers who are
temporary as stars.

Shame Go In Thy Company

Husband,
hard-boned and bearded, my
bearer of arms,

when the wind from the north woke you moaning
I knew everywhere of you,
landscape I was queen of:
queerness of that exile now.

With dawn light you ride home,
return exhausted,
refuse to look me in the eye

and I smell my own kind on your flesh,
in the palms of your hands:

forced or willing,
I know both~

as she, that one
you crossed by moonlight
like a river border,
like tearing water.

Foray

Elsdon Churchyard

Elsdon Churchyard

Full-termed they were,
bald pated.

Each one I named ~ my Thomas,
my Hobie, my Robert and my John.

Their father called me *witch*,
kicked at my congregation,
pale as mushroom in the brown and benty ground.

Hush, I told them, *hush*.
Let it be so. Heft,
shift. Be still now.

On Hopeburn Haugh

Behold the lilies of Hopeburn Haugh field : the little ones
who chew no meat
and who never grow old

Snub-petalled tooth in my lap
from a hoard long lost,
new found:
coggly dice to clash between my palms
or let lie still: morsels of bone,
little hard pillows.

Man now, the son
who bit me,
gulped my milk pinked with blood
when his jaws flamed, puppy-sharp,
in the smeddum
of this first coming.

Into its rootlet,
soft hollow, brown as apple core,
I fit the tip-end of my tongue
as a snail inside its shell,
as an eye into its socket,
as a blue egg, in time, its nest.

Book of Esther

Child then,
I sat cold in church, eyes closing
as the minister spoke
of fine white curtains, fluted and fluttering,
and so we flew, Esther and me, in each other's arms
through those long starry nets awash
with lilies of the morning.

Father stood afterwards by the doorway
honing his sword-edge on its stone
making ready for that night's ride.
The near-blunt metal
sounded a dreary grind along well-used grooves.
And the minister kept his counsel.

Esther, dance with me again, wrap me
in mists and evening clouds airy to the skin,
I want to be lifted through light,
lithe waves fine as a young girl's hair
to veil and unveil us.

Swifts

While I labour, bent
among bog-mud
clearing stone and clods
as if parting the Red Sea

they swoop like arrowheads
mocking my lone and earthbound body
with their effortless choosing
to stay or to go ~

I'll lob this rock
into their blue world that has no walls,
may it find its own true bride
in the airy oval of a skull

to marry in the morning
as I will never:
my wedding sheet his winding sheet,
he in his narrow bed and I in mine.

Our Lady Of The Midden

Early, I tend her. Attend her. She is patient, insatiable.
I bring her licked-thin wishbones, a cat's corpse, the spat-out,
soiled, marrowless unmendables of us.

Wide-shouldered on her ample haunches she is fine,
proud of her dirty, stew-dark skirts sewn with maggoty
pearls, she is multitudes, she multiplies.

The black-hearted hive of her accrues hourly and without cease.

She reeks, gamy, stinging: I entrust her with all that we are
in this world, all that is fouled, scabby and unclean
to the world's eyes, all we have that is holy.

Piss and spittle, bones boiled and boiled again
to sludge, leather grown thin and grey as spiders' web,
blood-packed clots of moss from our women's bleeding.

Our hunger and our want. Our joys
and secrets. She works, reduces.
She accepts.

Let the Wardens and the priests mutter over their clean page
and their cross: even their shit nourishes our earth.
Morning after morning

I come to the dense, slick back of her,
my living, breathing mother
who turns to offer me the hot throne of her breast.

My Minnie

Gone long
but minded,
my minnie:

I saw you in the fire, you sang
stories: *wheesht*
you'd whisper, *wheesht now*:

dreary days, grey, drear days go by,
the fire sits in its own ashes,
a sodden howl sticks in my throat:

days you are gone
as if you never breathed
and I, crossing mile upon mile of waste

or moor, the bordering hills
between two seas,
was never born of you

my minnie
but dropped on a borrowed wind,
your homing spirit

Foray

Catcleugh, January

Catcleugh, January

Some of winter is true. A clean yell

carrying through blue air,
black bark in its sleeve of snow.

Some rest in saying we have come

so far ~ while the still eye, cold,
holds us, scours us.

The midden is wonderful with stars.

World-stopped, we do not dream
or grow old,
we are like hares, forgetting
each print as we make it,

though it is beautiful, that path.

The Singer At Low Roses Bower

Past midnight as the dancers, flying,
fall slowly back to earth
and settle, light-headed as dandelions
while he stands, time turning quiet, and begins his singing.

Alone among them, listening, I am an open field,
I am swaying, soft rushes,
let him slit down and pull away this stiff green casing,
draw out the inward pith

to dry me white in summer's weightless air :
let him set me in a dish
for one November evening such as this,
a solitary wick in its sheepfat circle,

let other dancers weary
when he strikes the flame,
I will warm his throat's ache, I will let
my light hold him while I live.

Left Handed Kerr

Seventeen's grace
a flash in his fire-the-braes eyes,
skin sweet as the whin in early spring,
hair blue-black as a jackdaw's feather,

Crafty-minded, my Kerr
swift in the saddle and skilful
in the turning home of a hundred head,
stealthy and quick and sure:

Fierce Kerr, who got the king's displeasure
riding with Buccleuch, to come back
marked and wounded on our wedding-eve
forbidden to be married:

So May's rain was to be my fine-jewelled veil
our vows whispered in an empty church
but hours before the soldiers came I had a lifetime
learning him, the routes and hidden places

Memorised, mosses and high pastures, muddy
wet marshlands, the secret ways through hills,
cloudberry, thorn, butterwort and myrtle, scent of the wind,
the soft rush in meadows of timothy and speedwell

Then and always mine to travel,
no border or wall to hinder me, only
our own land, stark and dear,
its lone horizon.

Earth to Earth

Let not a child sleep upon bones
lest your tongue cut your throat

the bait hides the hook,
a word spoken
is an arrow let fly,

and you can have no more of a fox
than his skin.

So tell not all you know,
for the stars burn us where we are.

Foray

From here the darkness has us both:
new moon, hills and a few lit windows
small as buttons on a man's coat.
Dark has deep pockets and swirling folds of stuff.

Only the silver river of his parting
the unsteady muster of his substance
tell me he is moving. He is not
the clumped shape of a sleeping beast,

not the stick and stone fencing,
the then and now. Only the soft skin
membrane between.
I track him as if he were my pulse,

we are that close.
The dark thins between us.

First Light

My life for the price of a mare,
some yearling, scabby,

'Spare me' sticks in my throat.
When first light comes again

I'll have to mend what I can,
want for what I can't,

begin again, alone,
put down a stob or stake,

huddle the bairns round, stop their crying. Thole
till Candlemas.

Love, Love Decays The Body

A long road back
to where I swallowed the sword
that set me alight, a shooting star's
white burn, a scorch like whisky:

a long way falling
to my ashy place, windows small,
stairs curled tightly, the brand not tender now
but my familiar:

the making of love,
the using of,
can it be sewn or sealed, its own
undoing?

The hawk hovering
the men in long boots, lying down,
the scissors
and the sewing~

at the long end of a rope
swing song, wind song
unsung, unlearned,
moss, raw, scar,

blackfaced sinners all,
rattling the snow in their throats
their star-grit in my blood~
let them be forgiven:

let them be bereft:
I am bone cold
and mortal weary. Let morning come when it will
to cut or kindle.

Bird Cherry

Bird Cherry

What is longer than the way? Love.
What is whiter than the milk? Snow.
What is sharper than a thorn? Hunger.
What is rounder than a ring? The world.

Longer than the way
late May and heavy laden
she walks far in the woods, so far
she wearies and lies down,
the bird cherry's snowy sheets
kissing her bare skin
in breeze-born, goosedown drifts,
profligate and quiet
until she dreams
of the heart that set the two hearts in her to swell.
Whiter than the milk
she lies still as a hillside
one hundred years, then
stiff and cool, remembering, she shakes
the blossoms from her skirts,
steps on their soft curls and is forgot.

Sharper than a thorn
November clatters the bitter black fruits
fit only for starvelings.
Headlong, thrawn, she curses
branches shaken bald, her body's
used-up purse, the burn
at her breasts where wasps have sucked~
Rounder than a ring, the full moon
holds the new moon in her arms tonight:
snow falls on the bundle she digs
bare-handed to bury
in the bird cherry's cold lap.

A Death By Drowning

I am ready
I am ready
I am

open the latch, let the moon in
fleering from the moors where the clouds are lean
over my head slip a hood of worst
I'll not be the last, I've not been the first

I am ready
I am ready
I am

death, dress me in silver, cram pearls in my mouth
beads for the bride, for the widow a shroud
step to the river and halt where it's fleet
rope at my wrists and no shoes on my feet

I am ready
I am ready
I am

who took from who is a circle well-worn
there's never enough between meat and morn
but still the wide-mouthed bairns get born

I am ready
I am ready
I am

The Ash And The Alder

We danced silver-sided,
lightly, lightly, on this earth:
swans envied us.

Storm did it, suasive~
I first, but
 you, sister,
syne:

and so we go,
and sometimes slowly,
two passengers on a sea-facing journey,

we find we are in each other's arms
and my pale neck entwines with yours,
dancers who have left the dance, not to be parted now.

Kenspeckle

Outside by the byre, some
late hour at the turn of the year
or out on the brae, early,

on the drover's road
from a distance, the way
narrow, our gaze level

and now in the hen-house, hardly
breathing,
slipping in and out of my shadow;

(I know your limbs are weightless
and your mouth is a cave, I have ached
at the hip where you cup your hand)

you move
as if through memory, or water
rimmed with glow-worm fire,

taking on forms,
discarding them, in one light
a woman near death with the stare

of a small child;
in another, a girl
wearing my old face

Eggshell

At first murk I feed the midden.

Scourings fly from my hands, the scraped
slivers a hair's breadth from want
to enough. There's never plenty.

It is a musky rats' manger I nurse
most mornings; in worst times
even they hunger.

Underfoot the scutter and skitter of them as they flee,
their high bleat could be laugh or anger:
who knows what rats are to one another?

Maybe they pray, even, to their own saint,
to Dimas, that old thief, who repented on Calvary
or Helen, who gathers in the lost.

Look, Helen, at this, fox-taken:
dropped here emptied, a blue cap upturned
in ashes: turned again inside my hand

to a white-scoured skull of some unsuccoured reckling.

Dimas, you gave the Holy Family shelter
on their flight through Egypt;
Helen, comforter of women,

take this thing, femmer, crooked,
sunken as an old moon
turning inside out within the dark.

Heron

Last night I saw a heron flying
far and wide:
my man who should have lived
lies open-eyed, my man
who won't grow old and with me bide:
when next year thaws
they'll find my bones beside.

Spur

But will you stay
Until the day goes down

Twilight wraps us.
And hunger,
that makes of the dog a wolf.

You lie in my arms and grow younger
for I have a lifetime to remember
in the pictures flickering your skin.

Old hurts and wrongs I rub up
on the knot-twist-knot of your spine
till you rouse hot,

I clatter the spur in an empty dish.
That our enemies want
or want ourselves

is how it is:
smell of you on me,
on me the brand of your body yet.

Evestones

Each freckled the grass
warm as a fresh-laid egg, a fetched blessing,
a rocking heart calmed by its companion,
lifted and settled in our art or craft, to form
a word, snug in conversation.

Raised high, palm over palm,
handfasted from others' ruin
to garland our pillow,
we made these walls
as we made our children:

Now the weighing of my days
grinds me.
What purpose to the keeping out,
the holding in, no-one
but the curlew here?

I lie down in my dress of stone.
I will be unpicked,
in the crook of me
small things will shelter.
Mosses spawn. Memory not falter.

Foray

Wild, Perpetual Voice

Wild, Perpetual Voice

Only a peewit saw
how I began and where;
from high above, alone,
in swell of wind and far from home
neither north nor south yet far~
he passed over me, a cry
unheard, a scar unseen,
only his hollow bones and keen gulp of a heart
to ride the wide arc of the world
and I let him go, I tasted
the air and it was good.

All is done that we had ready: days' fullness falls
through hands, the steaming drench of them;
I stoop behind the plough, howking stones
till my knuckles split, my cheek's red raw
then stir the soup with my mother's spurtle.
Good on the second day, better on the third, best
yet when there's meat to it, not bones
or jealous wanting: the dree dregs of us, the spit
and spittle! Think neither sin nor shame, but mend,
make do, before the dead come haunting.

Too far from where I've got
to see straight now, I've salt in me, mingling
mothers of shallows and mothers of the deep.
And it rests me to imagine
how the unravelling begins.

First to rise, first to run, I hid
at their hooves' halt and, clapped
like a bird from a ditch, they trapped me,
remember~

Remember? If you remember you burn
and go on burning~

Wild, Perpetual Voice   2

A man's body maps his own dust,
rapes because he can and reives
because he must: does evil one day,
good another, as a dog chases its tail, the son
becomes the father.

Crossed and trampled,
I'll swill the mud from their boots, run on, run on
wayward, pinched sorely for it but never sorry!

By fire or sword we'll be clengit
and hangit, skeery and scabbit,
what can we do
but go on?

Our shape's the more debatable, a river
itself of borders,
blood in it that vanishes,
misted-over:

Who is this, who is this at our shoulder?

Pity us then, pity us all. Taste,
does it want salt? Three nights like the owls
on sour milk and stale meal:
"He that ordained us to be born
Send us more meat for the morn
Part of it right and part of it wrong
God never let us fast ower long".
~The whins prick us bare to bone.

Yet was that all of it? Remember?
My hinny and my heart, my dearies,
barefoot, berries in our apron?

Foray

Wild, Perpetual Voice   3

I run and run, no living thing can stop me

He slit, yes, with one cut, not to kill,
mixed the long spurt, steaming, into meal,
showed us how to stop its wound with moss.
Sour burn in my belly, mother.

**So young at the yowe-milking, up from Wintertown,
plenty laughing and doffing, songs and dances.**

**From further out, from this far away,
a life's twined branches form a thorn
or woman's braid. How can you follow,
cross and retreat, without forgetting?**

**Tup-heidit men telling stories of the hand-ba'
on Fastern's E'en, the fair day cockfights
and the kisses!
In the thick of it then, keeping the sides apart,
hem and edge ~ but where was I, between?**

*It's ewes make the heft of a hillside,
wean their lambs so they stay close, unstraying,
graze where their mothers' mothers stayed.*

Our men dancing their jigs on Harraby Hill!
Sick and like to die ourselves
we sewed sheets to wrap them in
but they never came home,
their unwashen hands, unwashen feet,
our name rots in the ground.
Ousen all, wedders and gimmers some,
and stirks we had, all gone.
Die and be done with you! Each day
shackled to the next and yet, yet, yet
the swirl of us, hard and sorry, as we come on!

Wild, Perpetual Voice   4

Hush: be with me now and at the hour:

**I love, I multiply, I lie down
in all I have made and all I have been,
all that has been done to me
meeting with myself here, at the end,
where the world begins.**

*Here and there the flow must rest,
thicken like milk and sleep, no use
one by one together:
who is this, who is this at our shoulder?*

All very well and all very well
but how am I to feed us?

A life's quick swallowed, aye.

*River that cuts through stone
while stone slept, and left
this ache in my belly, mother*

What can we do
but go on?

**For nothing is still, nothing is left,
nothing is lost**

**and so the bright drops of us
fly up**

Notes on the Poems

Who All names are of reiver battlefields, raids or strongholds, including bastle (fortified) houses and pele towers. 'Splent and sword' is armoury, a leather jack is a protective leather waistcoat sewn with metal plates worn by reivers. A Galloway was a small fell pony.

Alicia Unthank's Ark In G.M. Fraser's book The Steel Bonnets there is an account of a raid on the Unthank family in their farm at Melkridge in Northumberland. Alicia was the only member of the family present and the reivers locked her in a large store chest or 'ark.'

Truce Day, Kershopefoot Flat land on the border south of Hawick. It was where English and Scots prisoners were exchanged, and on Truce Days Wardens would meet here to sort out disputes. Fairs were often held on Days of Truce. The Tourneyfield at Kershope was a place of tournament where arguments could be settled by single combat.

Wake The words in italics are from The Book of Job.

Flight Before guns began to be more widespread towards the end of the 15th century the main weapons reivers used included swords, knives, pikes and most commonly the bow.

Eyebright Border communities, scattered as they were, used beacons to warn of impending attack. Sometimes women would spread sheets upon hedges and higher ground in warning. Eyebright is a flowering wild plant used for medicinal remedies including improving vision.

Howlet Stone 'Howlet' is a Northumbrian name for the owl, also called 'jenny hoolet'.

Shame Go In Thy Company The title is part of a line taken from the Border Ballad 'Dick O' The Cow'.

Elsdon Churchyard There are marks on the doorway of this church said to be made by reivers emerging from prayers and getting ready for a night's raiding by sharpening their weapons on the nearest stone surface.

Book Of Esther The first verses from this Book of the Bible describe flowing curtains. The poem refers to the sword sharpening at Elsdon.

My Minnie 'Minnie' is a dialect word for 'mother'.

The Singer At Low Roses Bower This was a well-known site in North Northumberland for dances and gatherings where ballads would be sung. Rushes were stripped, dried and used as wicks in sheep fat to make cheap lighting, candles of wax or tallow being something of a luxury.

Left Handed Kerr Robert Kerr of Cessford was a ruthless member of one of the foremost riding families. Born in 1570 he was riding by 15 and by 17 was engaged to the unnamed daughter of Maitland of Lethington. Taking part in a 2000 strong foray with the Lord Buccleuch and Lord Johnstone against the Collingwoods, he angered King James so much that he forbade Kerr to marry. The marriage did take place and Kerr was duly imprisoned next day. He went on to become Deputy Keeper of Liddesdale. The Kerrs were much feared and it is probably true that a great many of them were left handed since the spiral stairs built in their towers were 'back to front', suiting defence by a left handed swordsman.

Earth To Earth This poem is made entirely of old superstitions and sayings. The reivers were notoriously superstitious and believed in ghosts and spirits.

Bird Cherry The lines in italics are from a contemporary text : 'Riddles Wisely Expounded'. The bird cherry's blossoms are fragrant but its fruit is black and bitter.

First Light 'Thole' is to put up with, to bear. Candlemas marked the end of the reiving season, which covered the darkest winter months of the year.

Love, Love Decays The Body The title comes from a line in the ballad 'The Trumpeter Of Fyvie'.

A Death By Drowning Although the usual method of dispatching prisoners was hanging, women were more likely to be drowned. It was considered more 'seemly' and was also cheaper (less rope was needed).

Kenspeckle A Scots/northern word for distinctive, unusual, strange.

Eggshell 'Femmer' is a dialect word for fragile. St Helen was the reivers' patron saint, being the saint of lost things. St Dimas was also popular with reivers. He had been a criminal who was executed for thieving but who before his death found God.

Spur An enduring story is that the female head of the Charlton family set an empty dish with only an iron spur on it to tell her husband the larder was empty and he had to go out reiving once again.

Evestones A 'lost' village near Otterburn. Only a few stones remain to indicate that it was once a fortified village (like Wall, which is still inhabited) lived in by reiving families such as the Hedleys, Fletchers and Widdringtons, whose records of births, marriages and deaths are still kept in Elsdon Church. Apparently the inhabitants of Evestones were notorious for stealing from their neighbours.

Wild, Perpetual Voice The title is from a line in Judith Wright's poem 'River Bend'.
Many rivers, such as the Tweed, the Tyne, Esk and Annan, formed important crossing points and unofficial borders. A river has three ages, its source or youth, its full flow in middle age and its old age at the mouth or estuary like a human lifetime. In this poem three voices, belonging to one woman in her youth, middle and old age, speak sometimes to themselves, sometimes to each other.
Peewit: lapwing.
Spurtle: a short wooden stick for stirring porridge.
Dree: dreary.
Clengit and hangit: caught and hanged.
Skeery: strange.
'Three nights like the owls' is a quote from Mary Queen of Scots complaining that she had to live in a rough manner while visiting Bothwell's redoubt, The Hermitage.
'He that ordained us to be born…' is the reivers' grace.
Yowe-milking: ewe milking.
Wintertown: the reivers lived in more settled homes during the winter, down in the valleys, but during summer took their livestock up to higher ground and lived in makeshift shelters close to them.
Tup-heidit: a tup is a ram. Common saying for a stubborn man.
Hand-ba': a fast dangerous sport played at truce days and festivals. Forerunner of football which was also extremely dangerous in the 15th century when players were often seriously hurt.
Fastern's E'en: Shrove Tuesday.
Ewes make the heft of a hillside: generations of sheep use the same areas to graze. Ewes learn from their mothers where to set boundaries.
Dancing a jig on Harraby Hill: Harraby Hill lies just south of Carlisle and was the place where many reivers were executed. Methods of hanging were rough and ready and there was no drop or instant death so men were often said to be dancing a jig at the end of the rope.
Unwashen hands and feet: women would lay out their dead and part of this ritual was to wash the body. To go to the grave unwashed was to

suffer an unsanctified death.
Ousen: cows, wedders: wethers (castrated lambs), gimmers: infertile ewes (a term also used disparagingly towards women).
Stirks: a yearling, either bullock or heifer.
'Fye lad, fye, the gear's all gane': from the ballad 'The Fray of Suport'.

Sources

Bawcutt, P, Riddy, F., *Longer Scottish Poems 1375-1650* (Scottish Academic Press, Edinburgh, 1987)

Beattie W., ed., *The Penguin Poets: Border Ballads, 1952*

Grint, J., Bastles: *An Introduction to the Bastle Houses of Northumberland*, (Ergo Press, Hexham, 2008)

Marsden, J., *The Illustrated Border Ballads* (MacMillan 1990)

Godfrey Watson, *The Border Reivers* (Sandhill Press, 1974)

Moffat, A., *The Borders,* and *The Reivers* (both Berlinn, Edinburgh, 2007)

Reed, J., ed., *Border Ballads* (Carcanet, 1977)

Sadler, J., *Raiders and Reivers* (Ergo Press 2006)

Scott, W., *Minstrelsy of the Scottish Border* (Bannatyne, Edinburgh, 1803)

Sidgewick, F., ed., *Old Ballads* (Cambridge 1912)

Swinburne, A.C., Wise, T. ed., *Border Ballads* (The Bibliophile Society, Boston, 1912)

Watson, G., *The Border Reivers* (Sandhill Press 1974)

Also the songs and music, including contemporary and modern interpretations of Border Ballads, of June Tabor, Dick Gaughan, Sandy Denny and Johnny Dickinson